The Sixfold Path

The Sixfold Path

Six Simple Exercises for Spirital Development

JOOP VAN DAM

Floris Books

Translated by Otto and Dirkje Koene

First published in Dutch under the title
Het Zesvoudige Pad by Christofoor Publishers,
Zeist in 1996. Third edition 2007
First published in English by Floris Books
© 2007 Uitgeverij Christofoor, Zeist
English version © 2012 Floris Books, Edinburgh
All rights reserved. No part of this publication may be
reproduced without the prior permission of
Floris Books, 15 Harrison Gardens, Edinburgh
florisbooks.co.uk

British Library CIP data available
ISBN 978-086315-863-6
Printed and bound in Great Britain
by Martins the Printers, Ltd.

Contents

Preface

This book is about the experiences of people who practiced the six exercises of spiritual development. Rudolf Steiner first described these exercises in *How to Know Higher Worlds* and in *An Outline of Esoteric Science,* and it is advisable to read the two texts first. They are reproduced at the end of this book.

It goes without saying that their practicing was an individual activity. There was a need to share with others the difficulties and possibilities one experiences along the way. So groups came about where one could meet and exchange problems and discoveries on a regular weekly or monthly basis. This had a helpful effect and encouraged the perseverance of practicing. The experiences from these groups gave rise to this book. Those who wish to work with these basic exercises in a group will find a number of useful questions in Chapter 9.

Joop van Dam
Zeist 2011

Introduction

An increasing number of people feel the need for methodical self-development through spiritual exercises or meditation. What motivates them to make the extra effort this requires? Often the desire for self-development comes from feeling uncomfortable about the way we function in certain areas, for instance that our thoughts are a reflection of other people's opinions, while our own ideas have stopped flowing for some time. Or we observe that it is hard to control our feelings; they drive us along with them so fast that we are unable to retain them long enough to understand what they want to tell us. It can also happen that in our actions, all we do is react to what is happening around us. These observations can create such discomfort that we decide to do something to take command of the ordinary faculties of our soul.

Not just our own inner world but also the way we relate to other people can prompt questions, and we may find that there is some room for improvement in how we respond to others, and that in all situations we respond in a mature way. We may notice how hard it is to deal with people at work in such a way that no one feels excluded. Or in family life a certain routine can dull our experiencing new things together each day. In today's world, living in a community with others has become almost impossible without making this extra effort.

A third element prompting people to inner schooling is the growing desire for metaphysical experiences. This is particularly true of young people. This leads to the question of how we can school ourselves to become more objective, and prevent ourselves from entering a world of illusion, fantasy or selfish desires.

The sixfold path is not always easy to practice in a way that is effective. There are numerous circumstances that can prevent us from doing the exercises as planned. How can we keep fuelling our enthusiasm to persevere with this activity over a longer period?

One way that is helpful is to practice together with others. That way we can see that we are not the only one who has difficulty in sticking to the exercises and we can support each other. It also helps to look at our early and often clumsy developmental steps from a wider perspective. It was not until early in the nineteenth century that the whole concept of development started to dawn on people. Initially it was the Scottish geologist Charles Lyell who conceived of the idea that the earth went through different phases of development in the course of time. Darwin applied the idea of evolution to the kingdoms of the plants and animals.

It was only during the twentieth century that the idea arose of a psychological development in human beings. In the 1960s the awareness grew that each person can actively take up this developmental process. Today people everywhere are taking up this path of inner development. The awareness that we are on this relatively new road with so many others can be of help in fuelling our enthusiasm, energy and the persistence needed on this path of exercise.

1. The First Exercise: Control of Thinking

1. Control of Thinking

The first exercise of the sixfold path aims to control our thinking. It is advisable before beginning this exercise to read the description given by Rudolf Steiner in *An Outline of Esoteric Science.*

It is really quite evident why the exercises start with thinking, for we begin with that part of our consciousness where we are most awake, where our presence is most active. Only after we have become master here, can we descend to the deeper and less conscious layers of our being. We have to light the lamp of our thinking like a miner lights his lamp before descending.

Generally speaking, the quality of our thinking in our daily life is not very focused. If we look closely, we find that our thoughts often ramble widely. What we see around us, and our memories continually lead us from one association to another. The essence of this thinking exercise is to concentrate on one specific subject. We then check if we have successfully managed this. If we perform this exercise for five minutes a day over a longer period of time, let us say for a month, we will notice that our power of concentration and our objectivity in thinking increase.

How does this first exercise work? Rudolf Steiner recommended that we focus our thinking on an everyday object that has a clear purpose, and so allows us to easily verify the pictures we have of it: something like a cup, a spoon, a paperclip, or a match.

For some people it is helpful to choose a fixed moment of the day to perform the exercise. Others manage to employ the 'empty' moments of the day, for instance while waiting for a bus or train, making that time useful. At such a moment we withdraw from daily life for a short while; figuratively we close a gate between us and the outside world and enter our own inner workshop. Now we can turn our thinking light onto the chosen object.

We can do this in two ways. Either we place the chosen object before us, or we call it up in our mind from memory. In the second case, we will often be surprised how much more there is to observe when we look at the object in reality later. Having chosen a certain object, like a spoon for instance, we now carefully observe its characteristics: its size, its colour, its form and so on. To make our observations accurate and concrete, it can initially be a help to pretend that we are describing the object to a blind person.

The next step is not just to observe the object, but to develop thoughts about it. For this we have to ask questions. Asking questions helps lead our mind from associative thinking to focused, creative thought. I could ask myself (staying with our example): 'Why does a spoon have this form? What material is it made of?' Sometimes, to answer a question, it will be necessary to consult with others, or check in a reference book. This is not part of the actual exercise, but obtaining such information contributes to making our thought life real and to the point.

Like changing a tyre, it helps to have the necessary tools ready before we start. So it can help to ask a few questions before we begin the exercise. How is this object made? When was it made? Was it used previously for the same purpose? Does its name carry any significance?

Once we have done the exercise a couple of times with the same object — let us just stay with the spoon for the moment — we notice why the spoon has a given size and form, and what material it is made from. The 'idea' spoon is becoming visible behind its external appearance. By sheer observation of the object we arrive at a state of clear thinking.

If we have chosen the same object a few days in a row then we can arrange our thoughts in a more logical way. In the beginning, if we have difficulty in developing thoughts coming from our observation, it can help to choose a more complex object, like a bicycle, that consists of several components, each with its own purpose. In this way our initial thoughts can have a wider focus. Later we can move to a simple paperclip.

The important thing in doing this exercise is to stay with it for quite some time. When we begin, this is not that hard because our discoveries engender sufficient joy and energy to help our concentration. The object itself causes the interest, and keeps us focused. When the important initial discoveries have been made, and no new thoughts arise about the object, it becomes more difficult. We may feel tempted now to choose another object. However, the exercise becomes all the more meaningful and effective if we stay with the same object several more times. In some ways, the exercise now really begins, because now the concentration must come out of ourselves; creating the interest becomes our own activity.

Another problem we will have to face after some time is that our thoughts become routine. This expresses itself in speaking certain words automatically and without hearing them anymore or giving them further thought — for instance, hard, soft, hollow, sharp. It may be helpful then to replace our more or less dreamlike words into *mental movements*. Let me explain. Taking a sharp knife in our hand, we can say aloud the word 'sharp', but we could also mentally picture the quality of sharpness as a motion. We can occupy ourselves with 'sharp' as a process, as motion: sharpness separates, it cuts, it divides, thus carrying out as an inner action what the word indicates.

Which inner experiences can we gain by doing this exercise? In the first place we notice that our power to experience our own inner world, to live more in our inner world, becomes stronger. In a way we feel less dependent on the outside world and more self-supporting. As for our physical and mental state, we are better incarnated and thus more awake. Since we will be able to take active control of our movements more firmly, each time this results in our feeling comfortable and at ease. Our will has been mobilised in our thinking.

2. The Second Exercise: Control of the Will

2. Control of the Will

The aim of the second exercise is that we learn to manage the impulses of our own will. Putting it in a different way, the purpose of this exercise is to strengthen our striving towards taking our own initiative. Just as our thinking can be led by things we happen to hear or see, or by memories that spontaneously surface, so to a large extent our actions are an automatic response to inner or outer stimuli.

Often we can be very busy dealing with questions we have been asked by others, events we are involved in and to which we have to respond; we are ruled by our diary through the day and the week, or whatever. Many things we do originate outwith our initiative. A lot of our actions are simply reactions and not actions we have undertaken ourselves. There are situations that call on our willpower to exercise restraint, to consciously decide against doing something. Having finished reading the newspaper we could for instance decide quite consciously not to watch the television news. Conversely it can take a lot of effort to actually do something, overcoming some resistance, like going to a difficult meeting. In both cases we have been consciously working to control and guide our will ourselves.

This exercise requires us to decide at the start of the day or the previous evening to do something at a given time. Again Rudolf Steiner's original description is given at the end of this book.

What type of action can this be? Rudolf Steiner mentioned an 'insignificant' action. What he means by this is that the less the reason for taking the action comes from the outside, the harder it is to put into practice. It must originate from our own initiative. There is no need for the action to have an external effect, but that does not mean that the action must be meaningless — a misunderstanding that often comes with this exercise. On the contrary, through our thoughts while we perform the action, the action can become especially meaningful. For instance, we can have the intention to cross our arms at ten past three — in itself a meaningless action — but with the thought that such a gesture helps us to be wide awake. In a lecture Steiner offered the example of somebody who at a given time each day took seven steps forward and seven steps back again, thereby imagining evolution and involution. Here too it is the thought that gives meaning to the action.

Many people have difficulty in finding a suitable insignificant action. Rudolf Steiner once suggested watering the plants at a given time of the day as an example of this exercise. Soon after this, when he visited a house where several anthroposophists lived, he noticed people watering plants at given times. He was disappointed that his example had been carried out exactly as he had given it and that people had not been able to come up with their own action. For this exercise it is important to find our own action as this makes us use our own initiative.

We should take the word action literally. We must carry out something using our limbs. Even if we were to plan on reading three lines from a certain book at a given time, that would be a physical action because we have to take up the book and open it to read the chosen lines. Through the action we deliberately penetrate our will and our thinking with our self; this has an 'incarnating' effect. The other exercises are similarly down to earth. The thinking exercise takes an everyday object as a starting point and the third, fourth and fifth exercises are woven into daily life. Life itself offers the material that enables us to carry out these exercises.

What then is the purpose of fixing a particular time for doing the exercise? The significance is in exercising restraint. We have to hold back from carrying out the action until the right time. Holding off strengthens our consciousness, like water held by a dam rises to a higher level. Generally speaking, when we carry out an action as a result of our will, there is a lowering of consciousness. We sink, as it were, into the life of the will. The will is 'asleep' as Rudolf Steiner expressed it. Only after having completed an action can we judge whether what we did was good. By setting a time in advance for this exercise we have to keep it in mind until the moment of action. Having to wait is of crucial importance in training the will. At the right moment we can take the chosen action in full consciousness. It is as if we make an 'act' of it. This also helps overcome the resistance of our ordinary consciousness because on the face of it, these are insignificant actions.

The difficulties that present themselves while doing the various exercises are related to people's constitution. Some people have a remarkable talent for the will exercise; for others it is a hard task. No matter what they do, they do not manage to think of their planned action at the right moment. If that happens, we should not make it too hard for ourselves; particularly in the beginning we can use a shortcut. Doing inner exercises is just like physical training: if we overexert ourselves on the first day, we put ourselves out of action for quite a while because our muscles have to recover from the overexertion. It is the same with our will. By setting an objective that is too ambitious, our will becomes frustrated or even damaged. To begin with it is better to choose something that is not too difficult to give ourselves a reasonable chance of success. Some people who fail to do the exercise in the afternoon succeed if they set a time in the morning. What we can also do is to choose a time that coincides with a transitional moment, like the beginning or the end of a break, prior to or after dinner, getting on the train on the way home. Once that works, can we begin to choose times without external aids to alert us, for instance in the middle of a lesson, or while we are in a meeting. In such a situation it is helpful if we imagine the specific moment ahead of time and vividly picture the possible situation. We may also need to make some arrangements to facilitate carrying out the action, like making sure the booklet in which we want to write something is within reach.

Experience shows that succeeding with this exercise is something enjoyable. At the same time our physical vitality increases. If we are unsuccessful with this exercise and we continually forget the time we have set, our will may become paralysed. In that case it is better to carry out the action anyway, even though it is after the planned time, thus using our will. We will find after some time that our action will be closer to the chosen time. We also complete our planned task, and finishing something gives energy. Joop den Uyl, the Dutch prime minister in the 1970s, was once asked where he found the strength to do everything that went with the office he held. He replied, 'My energy comes from the things I finish.'

The will exercise is an appointment we make with ourselves. In general it is much easier to keep appointments with others, for we keep these appointments out of respect for the others. We can find the motivation to keep our appointment with ourselves by experiencing that our will can work independently of the outside world. When that begins to happen, our will has started to become autonomous.

3. The Third Exercise: Control of Feelings

3. Control of Feelings

The third exercise helps to train the world of feelings. It ensures that we do not *become* our feelings, but *have* feelings and to learn how to use these as a way to perceive ourselves and the world.

While doing the first three exercises we are, as it were, looking over our own shoulder to how we use the faculties of our soul. We look — as an outsider — at our own thinking, will and feeling. In doing the first exercise we may be surprised to discover how inconsistent our thinking can be. Doing the second exercise makes us realise how few actions we perform using our own initiative in our full and busy life. However, looking at the world of our feelings is the hardest. While working with groups of people I have noticed that this exercise gives rise to an inner protest: is it really necessary to control our feelings? Is it wrong to let our feelings run freely? Would such an exercise not dampen feelings? If we look at our feeling life, it seems at first as though we hardly have any feelings. Shortly thereafter many painful, if not negative, feelings appear to live in our soul; the number of harmonious, positive feelings we can identify is very small. It is this observation that causes the protest. However, it is worth enduring this observation; it increases our self-knowledge.

A first step in the as yet unfamiliar area of feeling is to make an inventory of the feelings we have had on a given day. In doing this, it is helpful to take a sheet of paper and literally chart the feelings we have had in the course of the day, as if it were a garden or landscape: a large field of irritations; a valley of doom, a little cluster of gratitude, a small bed of respect and so on. The map that evolves can vary from day to day, even though specific elements will return time and again. Once we have observed our feelings in this way for some time, we may discover that there is still another, secret garden inside us that hosts feelings that are obscured by more powerful feelings standing in front of them. This garden consists almost entirely of tender feelings, like the mood the blue of the sky evokes in early spring, or the feeling that we may have when entering a room with an open fire in winter.

Rudolf Steiner said that this third exercise concerns the expression of our feelings. This clears up the misunderstanding that this exercise might result in suppressing our feelings and removing spontaneity. It goes without saying that it is good to cry in cases of sorrow, and to laugh when there is joy in our heart. These feelings should not be pushed aside, but we can direct them in such a way that we do not drown in our tears or lose ourselves in laughter. What matters is that we acknowledge the feelings within us, identify them and give them a name. That way they become part of us and accessible. If we then take our feelings to the outside, we can be their companion and guardian. In this way we can not only express our feelings but also allow them to work inwardly. That is to say, we can try to observe what it is that the feeling wants to express. We may for instance notice that there is unrest in our soul and we can try to see where this is coming from. We hold the feeling and seek to look through it, as if it were a window.

It is our feeling that connects us with the world. Once we have discovered this bridging role of our feeling life, we can soon notice that there are two paths running over this bridge. An impression coming from outside evokes a feeling in our inner self. A skipping child, for instance, can give rise to a feeling of lightness. Thus a message of the world is carried onto the soul. Conversely, it can be the soul that initially tells us something. The memory of a teacher we had difficulty with as a child and who often wore green clothes can cause the colour green to arouse a feeling of antipathy in us. In other words, not only can a feeling tell us something about the world outside, but also about ourselves. If we manage to keep these two aspects apart, feelings can lead to knowledge of the world around us and also to knowledge of self.

Becoming conscious of our own world of feeling makes some of us discover that we have strong emotions, and others that our inner experiences are weak and take a long time to surface. In both situations something is out of balance. Probably each person carries both aspects within him or herself, and it depends in part on the outside world as to which aspects show up.

In doing this exercise, the strong emotions particularly catch our attention and it is their expression that we seek to control. But it is equally fruitful to foster the dreamlike, barely noticeable feelings. It often takes a while for this process to grow and we have to create the inner space for it. Placing this in the perspective of the 'feelings garden': some forceful feelings ask to be trimmed and pruned; conversely the tender feelings only develop when the seeds are tended and given space. Many strong feelings announce themselves and are unmistakable; they cannot possibly be overlooked. We have to become attentive of other feelings, listening carefully to them, like the mood that snow evokes, or a rainbow, a spring shower, or the beginning of autumn. The atmosphere in certain places is another example, how different the mood is of one city compared with another, or how different the atmosphere is at a nursing home compared with that at a school.

When doing the feeling exercise over time, we can take several steps. The first is to map a 'feeling garden' described above. The second step is to be the gardener of our soul and trim the feelings that are too loud, and tend the seeds of our quiet sensations. Having done this for a few weeks, we can take the next step: expressing our feelings. We are not accustomed to utilising feeling as a means of communication. In most cases what we experience is 'packaged' in the form of a thought. Not 'I am angry', but 'what you say makes me angry'. With the first we simply state the feeling, while the second is a judgement.

A feeling that has not yet hardened into a judgement but is

worded as a pure experience, presents an inner movement that can grow. An expressed feeling is always in a stage of growth. In taking it outside us, deeper levels of our feeling can be born. Another person can understand us better that way and with less bias. In doing so a fourth step becomes visible. The way we can help ourselves to become more aware of our inner motions, by expressing them carefully, is by listening without prejudice to another person expressing their feelings, and perhaps asking some questions. Obviously this last step cannot be taken until after we have reached a certain skill in the preceding steps.

There are few areas so conducive for feelings to thrive as the realm of art. That goes as much for creating art as for experiencing it. Actively experiencing art always happens through feeling. If we look for fifteen minutes at a piece of art, we may notice that quite distinct feelings have awoken in our soul. And if we are artists we will be guided by our feelings. If playing a sonata of Chopin, our feeling tells us at what speed to play and where the emphasis lies. Feeling then becomes an instrument in the true sense of the word.

The feeling exercise is a matter of finding the right balance. When Rudolf Steiner speaks about 'equanimity', it does not mean that you have to temper your feelings or suppress them, but instead, in spite of the rolling waves of emotions, you stay upright and in balance. With feelings you always have to deal with polarities: with comfort and discomfort, joy and sadness, sympathy and antipathy. One carries the other; one also enables the other to come to fruition. The tender beauty of a birch makes it possible to experience the robust power of the oak. This mutual balancing also applies to the relationship that exists between powerful emotions that involuntarily arise and have the tendency to become exaggerated, and the 'quiet' side of our feeling life, for which we have to create space. If we succeed in tempering the forceful and rapidly rising feelings, we save energy for the hidden and tender motions of our feelings. And the reverse also applies: feelings of devotion or reverence for religion or nature can balance the powerful emotions.

Contrary to the two previous exercises we cannot fix the feeling exercise to a particular point in time. What matters is that we grasp the moment at which the feelings arise and to ensure that we not only express these feelings but also allow them to work inwardly. At the start of the day, just before we step into the morning, we can pause and plan to carry out this exercise during the day. Looking back at the end of the day shows us the moments where we succeeded, or where we missed an opportunity. Looking as an outsider at the feelings that presented themselves during the day is an aid to have the presence of mind needed to catch the precise moment when they presented themselves. Through practice we can learn to live in the present. Our communication with the world, the breathing between the inside and the outside world is strengthened.

4. The Fourth Exercise: Positivity

4. Positivity

Rudolf Steiner described the basic exercises of spiritual training in a specific sequence. It is fruitful to observe this sequence. The preceding exercises are beneficial for the ones that follow and it becomes apparent that the sequence makes sense.

This can be seen when considering the legend Rudolf Steiner retold to illustrate the exercise in positivity (see p. 92). On one of their journeys, Christ and his disciples see a dead dog on the side of the road. The disciples shy away with horror from the decaying cadaver. In doing so they respond to the feeling that arises in them. Christ, however, goes a step further. He does not turn away from the dog, but observes and points to the shining white teeth that are not subject to decay.

This legend shows how first the disintegration of the dog's body is experienced, and because of this the integrity and purity of the teeth could be seen and appreciated. The fourth exercise builds on the experiences of the third exercise but takes a new step.

The first activity when doing the exercise in positivity is to persist and intensify our observation. We seek to strengthen our interest in the world and independently of the feelings that first arise. Very easily these feelings, particularly if they are negative, detract us from further observation. We no longer want to have anything to do with something that arouses such feelings. The expression, 'Stop the world, I want to get off', summarises it. Experience shows this attitude is unfruitful. We need to direct our attention and look for something that is positive. For instance, a teacher may be able to find in a messy child's drawing a tiny part which is beautiful and has come out well, through which other parts of the drawing are lifted to a higher level. Or looking at a notorious troublemaker in a group, we may often discover that this is just the person who contributes most to transforming the group into a community with a collective will.

The intention of this exercise is not that we no longer notice what is negative, but that in a negative situation we seek to identify the positive element. Walking through the countryside, we might be disturbed by the sound of a low-flying jet, but after this we can 'hear the silence'. This exercise strengthens our perceptions. A new and joyful voyage of discovery commences.

Next to this situational positivity exercise that is practiced in the moment itself, there is yet another, more long-term form. There are many circumstances and events in the world — and also perhaps in our own life — which cause abhorrence and which we'd rather not face. It often takes much effort before we are able to identify something positive in such a situation, to which we can say yes with conviction. In the Old Testament there is the story of Jacob wrestling with the angel, where Jacob says, 'I will not let you go before you have blessed me.' This blessing often only comes in a given situation if we have discovered something that inspires us, something that has a positive side. Then we can enter the situation again with conviction.

Also in more everyday experiences the positive cannot always be found immediately. The battle with the angel seldom lasts only a short while. We may find the positive only at the end of the day, if we make a point of looking back through the day. Often what upset our daily program and annoyed us at the time, later results in something new developing. In some situations it can be days or even years before we perceive the positive and experience this as a 'blessing'. This helps us to a better long-term perspective.

Part of the technique of doing the positivity exercise is to look back through the day at its end. This is often necessary so that we can see a new, fresh point of view in a situation that, at the time, we experienced as negative. Having found a new perspective after further reflection often creates a feeling of gratitude. It offers a new value to a past situation and at the same time gives us energy for the future. With practice we will be able to do this increasingly in the moment itself.

Rudolf Steiner calls the positivity exercise a basic one combining thinking and feeling. Feeling, which has gained in equanimity through the third exercise, is now used to relate to the world with a greater level of interest. Or one could say, after the negative aspects in the world have caused antipathy in ourselves, we now endeavour to make a conscious effort with high expectations of discovering the positive. As soon as we find this, thinking gains a new vantage point. It is the connection between thinking and feeling which opens a new approach to the outside world.

By finding such a new relationship, situations that have stagnated and turned sour can begin to flow and move forward. This new-found movement can give rise to a feeling of gratitude. It adds a new value to a past situation and creates energy for the future. The way to the future is thus made free. A wonderful example of this was demonstrated by Gorbachev when, during his presidency, he was asked about the miner's strike. 'They are right, considering their circumstances. And I am glad that they are striking. It means that the glasnost is gaining momentum. People are becoming independent.' Catastrophic as it was for the economy, Gorbachev had seen the positive side of this action. This opened the way for a meeting with the strikers.

In *How to Know Higher Worlds,* Rudolf Steiner describes the fourth basic exercise as learning tolerance. This gives a social dimension to the positivity exercise, because tolerance is an inner attitude. To tolerate someone, as well as accepting their negative characteristics means learning to see their positive qualities. The essence of the other is not in what they lack, but in what they have. Instead of simply disengaging ourselves from a situation because it annoys us, we can try to relate to it. In a relationship conflict, for instance, we can try to find an area where we can meet the other. In doing so, we take the given situation seriously. The reality consists of the others, the circumstances and ourselves. The positivity exercise is an exercise of inclusion. The given situation is seen as a question to us. By starting to look for an answer, we begin to relate to the situation, showing that we feel a responsibility towards it.

This exercise has a liberating effect. We will no longer be drawn so easily into a difficult situation because we counter it with a free, inner deed. Our extra activity creates the atmosphere that allows others to be liberated from being locked into a situation. Even some humour might break through. We find a new point of view on another level.

5. The Fifth Exercise: Open-Mindedness

5. Open-Mindedness

Open-mindedness is an ability that young children possess naturally. Infants and toddlers show the spontaneous ability to experience every moment of the day as new. What comes naturally when we are young must be practiced later on with much effort. The exercise of open-mindedness is not an easy one. The more knowledge and skill we develop during life, the harder it becomes to have an open mind. We have to again acquire 'the innocent eye of the child', as the English art critic Herbert Read recommended when looking at art. It is a gift to be able to see something new each spring when seeing the first snowdrop. Abraham Maslow calls on us to 'appreciate again and again, freshly and naively, the basic good of life'.

Rudolf Steiner characterises this fifth exercise in the series as an exercise for thinking and will combined. Out of both something new must be born. In other words, what we know (thinking) and what we can do (will) we set aside for a moment in order to be completely open for what may come our way.

Knowledge, judgements, opinions, as well as skills can lead to a form of imprisonment. They can prevent us from perceiving things differently, from making fresh judgements and taking a different approach. Often we barely realise how our judgements are coloured by concepts and events from the past, nor do we notice how much past experiences have formed our habits and control our present ways and actions, for instance the way we react to people we know well. Once we become more aware of this, we see that in many situations our thinking and our actions stem from a certain pattern. Having an open mind means that we set ourselves free from such imprisonment.

We can also describe this in a different way. As we gain greater insights, and as we gain our own experiences and develop skills, our awareness of our self grows. In this internal processing of our experiences, our 'I' has its foundation. Having our own frame of reference offers inner security. Understandably as time passes we become attached to these reference structures. The exercise in open-mindedness demands that we have the courage at some point in time to set aside this frame of reference. This may call for a little self sacrifice.

How does this exercise work in practice? Initially having an open mind means holding back judgement. For instance, if we meet somebody who is unemployed, we do not immediately start to guess why they are unemployed. We must endeavour with all that we encounter, to preserve an open mind, an observant attitude for as long as possible. This attitude will allow the world to express itself as comprehensively as possible before we begin to say something ourselves. This attitude is reflected by what Willem Zeylmans van Emmichoven once said: 'If people were to judge a little less, how much they would find.' The morphologist Dick van Romunde advised us to learn to 'be silent', that is to be *actively* silent. Holding back judgement is part of the thinking component of the exercise of open-mindedness.

The will component lies in what is called trust in *How to Know Higher Worlds* (see page 88). 'We must learn to approach every person, every being, with trust. Such trust or confidence must inspire all our actions.' The open-mindedness of small children expresses itself in the urge to imitate. With absolute trust children imitate everything in their environment. When they are six or seven years old, this natural imitation urge diminishes. With the awakening of the ability to perceive one's own inner world an early form of self-confidence is born. Much later, starting from the middle phase of life, a different relationship to the world starts to grow: trust or confidence comes back in a new form. It is a confidence in life, a confidence in destiny based on the conviction that in meeting the world — even if it is not harmonious — there is always something new that can be discovered and developed.

In training our feelings as well as with the positivity exercise, we saw that looking back at the events of the day is a help to become more awake for the moments that require these two activities. In terms of being open-minded, looking back can also be a valuable aid. We can ask ourselves, for instance, which 'wonder' has happened during the day. Surprisingly, there is always something that can be found. People who have a tendency to take life too seriously often develop a new trust in life by discovering the wonder that occurs every day. Recognising at the end of a day that we are connected to the world, allows us to meet the following day with a more open mind.

The art of being open-minded is often experienced as the most difficult single exercise to carry out. Three ways can offer some initial access to this basic exercise.

The first is perception. What is it that a pure sense experience can tell us, like an odour? It is important not to immediately connect it to experiences from the past, to a memory, and say: this has the smell of a rose. Doing that we would not find anything new; it is like saying poverty is caused by the lack of money. What can help is to make a pencil drawing of what this specific odour 'does'. Lavender has a different gesture than the odour of rosemary. Lemon has an entirely different gesture again. If there is a group of people and each person draws a picture, it is interesting that the characteristics of the various odours show a resemblance. There is indeed an element of objectivity in the perception. Similarly we can find what impact colours have on the soul. What does the purple of amethyst, the red of carnelian and the blue of aquamarine express? There as well we may find objectivity. If people describe these qualities in one or two words, they will be very close together. Sometimes even a profession may be named that epitomises these qualities.

The second doorway to open-mindedness uses another soul power. Perception stems from the upper part, from the head. In the limbs, the lower part, action and will are vested. Open-mindedness can express itself there in spontaneous actions. We might call this an unintentionally successful act. If we look back at the end of a day we may discover that in the midst of a difficult situation we acted in a way we had not thought of. For example, a teacher crossed the road with her young class to play a game in the park. An overactive boy did not stay in line but ran all over the place. On the way back the teacher decided to pick up the boy and carry him on her shoulders. The boy immediately became quiet and said, 'I can see everything from here; I can even see the school. If one of the children steps out of line, I'll tell you.' Later it occurred to the teacher that having the overview relieved the boy of his unrest. If we begin to become aware of these types of unintentionally successful acts that occur regularly in life, we can benefit from them.

The third doorway lies between the poles of head and limbs in the middle area of our heart and lungs. In breathing we inhale the world and exhale it again. In our heart lives the force of empathy that creates a warm, inner bond with the world. It is in this realm that encounters take place. It is an art to deal with what comes to us from the world, and to do this with an open mind. The world constantly offers us situations through which we can develop further. These possibilities stem from the future. The open-mindedness of the centre lives in our ability to receive what destiny brings us, and to say 'yes' to this, and then to deal with it in full awareness.

When doing the first three exercises, we are, as we have seen, looking over our own shoulder at how we work with thinking, will (doing) and feeling. In doing so, not only do we exercise and refine these powers, but we also strengthen them. This increased strength is used in the fourth exercise in linking thinking and feeling, and in the fifth, linking thinking and will. When it becomes hard to practice positivity and open-mindedness, our experience is that it helps to resume doing the first three exercises again. In this way we increase our strength to better carry out the fourth and fifth exercises, giving them a new lease of life.

Just as the positivity exercise offers a new viewpoint of the world, so exercising open-mindedness allows the openness to look at things from *all* vantage points. Our attitude toward the whole world becomes full of expectation. We are not just learning to see, but also to listen. Positivity relates to open-mindedness as seeing does to hearing.

Open-mindedness finds its source in the trust that each day we can develop and renew ourselves. We become interested in the word each day anew. *Le monde commence aujourd'hui* (The world begins today) is the title of a book by Jacques Lusseyran in which this open and expectant relationship to the world is described. The courage it takes to embark on this adventure awakens a rejuvenating power in the soul.

6. The Sixth Exercise: Harmony

6. Harmony

In the course of outlining the five exercises that have been dealt with, we haven't discussed for how long one has to keep doing a given exercise for it to have a fruitful effect. In his book *How to Know Higher Worlds,* Rudolf Steiner writes that the inner activity these exercises require will ultimately lead to acquiring qualities such as positivism, equanimity and the like. He also used to say, after explaining an exercise: 'And in the course of time that must become a habit.' It takes about a month to learn a new habit. To begin with, each exercise can therefore be practiced over a period of four weeks.

Having discussed and practiced the five basic exercises, we move on to a sixth exercise. This consists of joining the previous exercises into a harmonious whole. We can focus on practicing two exercises for a while, such as the third (the feeling exercise) and the fourth (positivity) which are interrelated. Alternatively we can take the first and the fifth — the thinking exercise and practicing equanimity — and devote a month to this. In the course of time, the combinations can be expanded, and that way the practice gradually evolves into a comprehensive whole.

If we want to understand the sequence of the exercises, it helps to look at how the exercises relate to time. Soon a structure becomes visible. The first two exercises, those of thinking and will, form a relationship to the past. The thinking exercises focus on objects that are complete. They originated in the past: at some point somebody designed them. With our thinking we trace back to the moment of their origin. The exercise of the will has a relationship with the past. We decide beforehand on a moment to carry out the action. The exercise of the will is primarily an exercise that works with the element of time. We can notice that we experience the different qualities of the day in a different manner. In carrying out decisions we took in the past, we connect ourselves with the current of time flowing from the past to the present. That is the element of time that can be calculated and controlled.

The feeling exercise, the third exercise, focuses on the present. Of the three forces of the soul, thinking, feeling and will, it is our feeling that lives in the present. We cannot catch our feelings. They arise and grow in a real situation. The feeling exercise requires us to catch the actual moment at which the encounter with the outer world arouses and develops feelings. Catching that point in time means taking control of unduly strong emotions, or creating the inner space where tender feelings can grow. It is a now-or-never exercise.

In practicing positivity we step into the future. Negative feelings that occur at any moment challenge us to endure or tolerate them for a little while. In a given situation, we look for a complementary experience. If we find the positive element, it is possible to perceive the situation in a new way and embrace it. The extra effort opens the way to the future; we can move on again.

The positivity exercise, and even more the exercise of open-mindedness, help us enter into another time stream: the time coming towards us. The time flowing from the future originates in eternity; it is time without boundaries, time in which everything is still possible. Suddenly something unexpected happens, which ruins all the plans we have made. The challenge then is to look at the opportunities this new situation offers. An illness, an appointment that is missed due to a traffic jam, a surprising encounter, or some other event, can mark the beginning of a new direction in our life. At such a time it is crucial that we are open-minded and have the presence of mind needed to seize the chance given and that subsequently we have the courage to head in a new direction; confident that we will find the next sign when needed. In this way the five basic exercises are instruments that support our journey from the past, through the present into the future. At the same time when we combine the individual exercises into one, they create the capacity to connect the time coming from the past into a breathing relationship with the time that comes towards us with all the challenging opportunities this offers.

7. The Sequence of the Exercises

7. The Sequence of the Exercises

Experience shows that we are always called to order if we think we can carry out the exercises in a random order. However, it is hard to understand why the thinking exercise is followed by the exercise of the will instead of the feeling exercise. The feeling exercise would seem to be the obvious one. John Davy cast an unexpected light on the composition of the exercises. As a journalist at *The Observer* newspaper, Davy interviewed Elisabeth Kübler-Ross, a pioneer of terminal care. She told him about the five stages everyone goes through when confronted with the prospect of imminent death. After denial (this cannot be true; there must be a mistake in the outcome of the tests; it concerns somebody else) there follows a period of anger (why me?). The protest that surfaces out of the depth of their being is projected into their environment. Then a phase of negotiation follows (I will start a diet, stop smoking, make a donation to the church), in the hope of a reversal. Then comes a phase of depression in which everything seems hopeless. Finally almost everybody reaches the fifth phase; this consists of the acceptance: the inner preparedness to encounter death.

Once he had returned home, the steps Kübler-Ross had described seemed familiar to Davy. Pondering this, he recognised the relationship to the five basic exercises. The exercise which trains the thinking helps overcome the state of the denial (which concerns the very idea that one is going to die). Similarly the exercise of the will helps to direct the anger about the helplessness felt about the illness into the right channels. The feeling exercise helps to avoid falling back into illusions through negotiation. The positivity exercise creates the strength to ignite the inner light in the phase of the depression. Having an open mind helps to reach acceptance.

The connection between the five inner stages of terminal illness and the five basic exercises is very clear. They originate from the same sphere; they stem from one and the same reality. They show an inherent order. Kübler-Ross indicates that the different stages are always experienced in the same sequence (though sometimes there is a relapse into a previous phase) and no phase is ever skipped. Those who learn to live consciously with imminent death will necessarily gradually transform their inner self. Practicing the basic exercises is essentially going on the same path, but using our own initiative: through this inner activity we learn to dwell in a new way in other regions of our being.

The relationship to different parts of our being

Rudolf Steiner briefly outlined to Nora Stein-von Baditz, one of the first Waldorf School teachers, how these exercises relate to different parts of the human being. While on this path of exercises we undertake a journey through the parts of the human being. Steiner connects the thinking exercise with the 'use of the physical body'. A physical object is necessary for doing the thinking exercise. The observation on which the thinking activity is based eventually leads us to the idea that lies behind the object. The object is the physical embodiment of this idea.

The exercise of the will leads us to become 'conscious of the ether body'. The ether body is the bearer of life processes that take place in the course of time. With the help of the ether body the 'I' develops a sense of time. Our memory is also a function of the ether body. In the exercise of the will, learning to work with time plays an essential role.

Doing the feeling exercise involves 'getting to know the astral body'. This astral body or soul body has many aspects. When describing the feeling exercise I have used the picture of a garden with plants and shrubs. By the same token I could use the picture of a zoo. 'You must get to know all animals inside you in order to be able to tame them', the way the Little Prince did with the fox in the story by Antoine de Saint-Exupéry.

To do the positivity exercise, the fourth in the series, we need courage. The effort that is required to see things in a positive light becomes possible because the human being is an I-being. 'Experiencing the I' is how Rudolf Steiner typifies this exercise. When discovering a new perspective a light begins to shine in the darkness. From that moment on we hold the rudder in our own hand and become the captain of the ship of thinking, feeling and will.

When exercising open-mindedness, we go a step further. Rudolf Steiner characterises this as 'preparation of the spirit self'. Open-mindedness is learning to live with what we have to face. Life on earth is not only determined by our everyday 'I'; the world too plays an active role in our biography. Recognising this is the beginning of an awareness of destiny or karma. Part of our being encounters us from the future, waiting to be met by us. In his book *Theosophy*, Rudolf Steiner names the region in the spiritual world where we become aware of karma as the region of the spirit self. Just as acceptance enables us to take the step through the gateway of death, so open-mindedness opens the gateway through which the spiritual world can already be experienced during life on earth. Through the spiritual or higher self this objective spirit enters our conscious mind.

In the course of evolution new 'layers' have emerged in the human being. The basic exercises are aimed at the human being in his present constitution. With the sixth and last exercise the force is mobilised which brings the different parts of the human being into one harmonious interplay. At the same time an organ is developed in us through which we can perceive and encounter the world in a new way.

8. Motives for Schooling

8. Motives for Schooling

Until the age just prior to the beginning of our calendar, people were selected to follow a path of initiation. They were accepted into a mystery school because of their descent or on the basis of specific qualities.

In today's world the decision to follow a path of inner schooling has developed as an initiative that each of us can take in freedom. The word 'initiative' holds the secret of the modern situation: we take the first step ourselves. Every external force towards schooling would be a weakening of the nucleus that starts the process of change and sustains it. That nucleus is the 'I', the essence of the human being.

Different motives may prompt us to follow a path of initiation. I will briefly discuss three of them.

Striving for health

These days many people experience a sense of restlessness and disharmony in their soul. Daily life with its overload of information and its ever-increasing speed draws our attention to the outer world. The moments we can turn to our inner self are diminishing. If we seek to do this, we notice how hard it is to close ourselves off from the world and concentrate our mind on something else. If we are too open to the world, we are tossed from left to right and cannot disconnect ourselves at night from our impressions. The result is that our sleep is undermined.

Another source of instability can lie in our world of feeling. For instance we may experience things too strongly, and thus become unbalanced. Or — and this happens increasingly — we close ourselves off from our feelings as a protective measure in order to survive. The result is that there is a continual stress at the base of our consciousness, and our will can be damaged. This can express itself in feeling tired, but it can also be the case that we can no longer become active in our soul. The result of this is that we may feel depressed.

The condition of our soul has an immediate effect on our physical wellbeing. This century it has become known as psychosomatic medicine, or later as psychoneuroimmunology (PNI). The French author Jacques Lusseyran describes the two aspects of our inner being in his book *Against the pollution of the I*, or *What One Sees Without Eyes*. The first aspect he calls the *ego*. The ego is jealous, wants to be the best, wants to pull everything toward itself and is constantly engaged in gaining esteem. The other aspect Lusseyran characterises as the *self*. The self is 'an impulse, a movement which puts at my disposal my thinking, feeling and will'. The self does not want the world to come to us, but enters the world to encounter it. The self means 'richness in the midst of poverty, interest when everybody around us is bored, and hope when everything seems lost'. The ego is 'self-directed and works out of a shortage. The self is world-oriented and receives through this attitude to life extra energy in order to remain creative, even in difficult circumstances'. Lusseyran describes how in the concentration camp at Buchenwald he experienced this very clearly among the camp's inmates. Those who could draw from the strength of their inner self were able to establish a future objective and thereby often remained alive. People who no longer saw a future and stopped fighting deteriorated physically much more quickly.

In our daily life we all carry both aspects of life, that of the ego and that of the self inside us. Being self-centred is needed for our self-preservation. However, it is possible to increasingly develop an orientation to the world.

Broadening perception

A second motive for schooling shows itself as soon as we have arranged order in our soul and acquired reasonable health. This is followed by the spontaneous urge to develop the talents we carry. Abraham Maslow describes in his book *Motivation and Personality* how the need to act can originate initially out of a deficiency. Maslow characterises this as 'deficiency motivation'; actually these are the impulses which stem from what Lusseyran calls the ego. Once the shortages (of money, clothing, safety, getting attention, love, etc.) have been replenished, the possibility for growth motivation takes effect. The motivation to grow originates from the self. Our actions are no longer meant to fill a shortage, but to create new realities. Instead of the deficiency something extra, a surplus, arises; something new is added to the world. When this happens, this marks the beginning of what Maslow calls 'the self-realising human being'.

Each person possesses this potential. In most cases the two needs, the deficiency motivation and the growth motivation, play a role in people's lives. If the growth motivation becomes more prominent, certain inner attitudes appear. Maslow describes these spontaneously developing attitudes by looking at examples of who he considered to be self-realising people: Lincoln, Franklin, Emerson and Goethe. Typical of these people is that they shared a need to be alone from time to time; to reflect on what had happened, to think about values, to pray, etc. They were grateful for what life had brought them as joy, as pain and as suffering (positivity). Thereby they felt connected to the world, or as Maslow said, 'appreciated again and again, freshly and naively, the basic good of life' (open-mindedness). It is as if what is being pursued consciously by the fourth and fifth exercises (positivity and having an open mind) became a characteristic feature of people such as Emerson and Goethe.

If the self can use the powers of thinking, feeling and

will in this way, they can become instruments for perceiving inner, metaphysical realities. Gradually, this possibility is being generally accepted. There are a growing number of children have spontaneous metaphysical experiences. Near-death experiences are no longer seen as a psychiatric phenomenon. These kinds of experiences are mostly the preserve of those who carry with them from an early age a certain sensitivity or are constitutionally changed by some far-reaching external event like a serious illness, or a biographical shock. As a result, they have these inner experiences. This prompts the question, can we reach these experiences also through some activity that arises from inside? Is it possible to take conscious steps that will lead to the inner reality of the world around us?

We know our own inner reality, the world of our thoughts, feelings and will impulses. We can become more awake to that world by practicing seeing the relationship between certain thoughts and being able in this way to think in a more creative manner. We can also become more observant of our own moods or dreams, or become more aware of certain impulses. We then work in the area of intellectual laws, of feeling qualities and will directions in our own soul.

Not only our own soul, but the world around us, is full of wisdom, of qualities and intentions. It is possible to acquire the ability to see the spiritual reality outside our self. To that end however, we must school our thinking, feeling and will in such a way that they become organs of perception for the world of the spirit. With our thinking we perceive. Through the empathy of our feeling we can experience something of the being of another person. With our will we can sense what the world demands.

Community formation

A third schooling motive arises from recognising a new era of community forming. In earlier ages community relationships had a structure from above. The origin of this form of community is the hierarchic direction, which originally came directly from the gods, and then the representatives of the gods (the pharaoh, the pope, a priest). Belonging to such communities or groups or medieval craftsmen's guilds, demanded obedience to existing rules, but also offered protection. Their leaders offered protection against other peoples, other religions, incompetent competitors, and so on.

In our time another structure is beginning to develop alongside the structure imposed from above. As the individual becomes more assertive and independent, ranks, social hierarchy and the like become less obvious. A new principle is emerging where the direction does not come from the top, but from what is needed at the base and is carried in freedom. Managing such a structure requires the interaction of both principles (from top down and bottom up). If we wish to create something that belongs to all, it calls for a lot of effort. We can no longer step back and place the responsibility on others. At the same time there is the need to have trust and confidence in the developing capacity of others. We have to accept that growth of the other is only real if it is really wanted from inside. We also notice that we have a key position in this contemporary community's formation. Unless we acquire a new inner attitude, we cannot really expect anything from the other.

The six exercises and the three motives

For each motive the six exercises are used in a slightly different way. Sometimes we can begin to use the exercises as they are; sometimes we can adapt them.

Let us look at the first motive, striving to become a healthy person. Being able to *control our thoughts* is a powerful tool to help focus on our inner world. We learn to close ourselves off from the impressions of the outside world that tempt us to simply drift along and oppose us taking our own stance.

Controlling our will teaches us to develop a new relationship with time. We learn to do things at a time we ourselves determine. We can also adjust the will exercise to suit our circumstances. From time to time it may happen that certain upsetting feelings well up; we may feel guilty about something; we may be concerned about something or someone, or we may be afraid of some imminent event. The upheaval in our soul is quite right and we do not want to suppress this. However, these thoughts and feelings are not fruitful if they buzz our soul all day like a fly. In such a case, we can make the following resolve. 'Tonight at quarter past nine I will concentrate on the problem. I will try to relate to it in a new way and then I will stop after fifteen minutes and continue with this tomorrow at the same time.' We allocate a specific time of the day to the problem, and can attend to our other priorities for the rest of the day.

To acquire inner peace through the *feeling exercise* is an important step. We raise to a conscious level the feelings that float around within us, of which we are only dimly aware and which create discomfort, fear or irritation. In the exercise we focus on them by giving them a name. Once we become aware of our feelings they lose their compulsive nature. Then we can perceive them as messengers of our own inner world or as intermediary to the world around.

Doing the fourth exercise, *positivity,* helps us to see a negative event as a challenge to develop a new relationship to the world. Using our own initiative we can attempt to make something positive out of such an 'obstacle'. If there is nothing negative in our life, it does not necessarily give us a feeling of contentment. Once I asked an old acquaintance in passing, 'How are you?' He replied: 'I am feeling bad.' Concerned, I enquired why. 'Because I don't have any problems. The gods have deserted me!'

The *open-mindedness exercise* helps us to keep interacting with the world. It prevents us from closing ourselves off, isolating ourselves from our environment if we are not feeling well; this can have a paralysing effect.

The sixth exercise, *combining* the separate exercises, creates rest and balance in the soul.

With regard to the second motive for schooling, expanding one's perception, there are specific inner activities that focus thinking, feeling and will on the metaphysical world. They can be summarised under the common heading of 'meditation'. The exercises of the sixfold path are preparatory exercises for meditation. They carry within them the seeds, which in meditation can come to development and fruition.

Training our thinking lays the foundation for having the concentration and the practical objectivity to hold abstract content in our consciousness for a while.

Control of the will is an agreement we make with ourselves not just once, but for a longer period. Experience shows that this commitment is harder to keep than one made with somebody else. The schooling decision is one of the most important agreements that somebody can make with themselves. The second basic exercise strengthens the independence required for this decision and helps to intensify the commitment for a longer period of time.

The third basic exercise, *the feeling exercise*, eventually leads to our becoming masters of the world of our feelings. We begin to feel responsible for the feelings that — prompted by our encounter with the world — arise within us. Like a guard we watch our feelings and ensure that they go through a fruitful development.

The *positivity exercise* teaches us to remain upright in difficult or negative situations. We continue as it were to be master of what is happening. This is the case because we continually ask ourselves what is essential and what is not essential. In other words, what am I learning from this? That question is the guide that the 'I' uses to create the inner rest and peace that allows meditation.

In exercising *open-mindedness* we clean the window that faces what is coming towards us from the world, keeping the view to the future unobstructed. In everyday life it means that we develop an eye to see the chances fate deals us and to act on them appropriately. In meditative life it means that we are open to unexpected or inexplicable impressions. We learn to free our will and our thinking from all known experiences so that they can act as instruments of perception of the spiritual world.

The *all-embracing* exercise, where we practice all exercises, ensures that thinking, feeling and the will come into and remain in balance.

For the third motive, the will to actively stand in a community, the six exercises also offer concrete and direct help. Particularly in the description of the exercises given by Rudolf Steiner in *How to Know Higher Worlds*, the social aspect can be recognised at once.

Here I want to mention a way to work with the social element that becomes possible if we combine the basic exercises with looking back on the day. Rudolf Steiner describes how during an encounter between two people a process takes place that can be compared to falling asleep and waking up again. If one of them says what they wants to say, the other can be open for what is coming, if they are prepared to silence their own thoughts and feelings completely, that is to say, to let them 'fall asleep'. Generally speaking, someone can manage to do this for only a limited time. Waking up again consists of letting their own 'I' become active by expressing themselves. It can happen in a community that one of its members radiates such force that the others fully surrender themselves to his or her views and opinions. The danger is that they 'fall asleep' too much in relation to this person, and that they stay insufficiently 'awake'. The community would then consist of a smaller number of individualities because some people have let themselves go to sleep, as it were simply becoming a copy of the revered leader. In this way, dependencies come about. For a modern form of community formation this is an impediment. The reverse, however, can also form an impediment: if the breathing process of falling asleep and waking up never takes place and all members remain constantly awake. Nothing will then take place between them.

How can we encourage the process of falling asleep and waking up in a conscious way? Once we are alone, we can do this by looking back at the encounter and then preparing for the next. While looking back we are catching up with ourselves again. The review technique consists of three layers. The first is the outer appearance: what did everyone say exactly? The second layer is about the intentions: what did everyone do; primarily, what did they express by way of will impulses? The third layer is the question, what did I feel? Where did I feel a warming, where did I feel icy, what really touched me?

This exercise consists of the control of thinking, will and feeling combined with the review technique. In a community we may focus the review of the will, especially on the will of the *other*. We can the endeavour to help the intentions of the other to come about. Such an inner attitude facilitates community formation.

Reaching out and listening to other members of the group — falling asleep — can be practiced in the actual situation. The harder we find it to get along with the other, all the more important is it to do this. In a group there can be people who are stuck in certain parts of their being. Such people often show predictable reactions in a given situation. Normally such a reaction arouses negative feelings for the very reason that it is difficult to meet that 'stuck' part of the other on which he has no grip and therefore cannot develop.

Only if we can find something apart from this seemingly inflexible area will we be able to endure the negative. Relating to something that someone does have, is a 'falling asleep' a listening to the other. The other can then awaken, grow and express himself. This growth can often spread to their inflexible parts.

The open-minded exercise immediately connects to this. In a relationship with another person, having an open mind shows the conviction that there are hidden qualities within the other. In *How to Know Higher Worlds* the open-mindedness exercise is called trust. If we lose trust in someone, it can have a damaging effect on their further development. The converse is just as true. Confidence placed in another person is as vital to them as the sun is for a plant. Having trust or confidence in each other is an essential condition for a community. In being positive and having an open mind we train the ability to open ourselves to other members of the community. Just as doing the retrospective review exercise of our thinking, feeling and will is meaningful after a meeting, so positivity and having an open mind can contribute to preparing for the next meeting of the same people.

9. The Six Exercises and the Schooling Path

9. The Six Exercises and the Schooling Path

Rudolf Steiner addressed the exercises of the sixfold path in different ways over the course of the years. He spoke mostly of the 'six characteristics' or 'virtues' that must form the foundation of every spiritually-oriented schooling. Through the exercises we gradually build the basis on which to work on further inner development. This is why they are called *basic* exercises. It goes without saying even without further spiritual schooling, they have an intrinsic value for life.

Parallel exercises

It is interesting that Rudolf Steiner describes the basic exercises not just as preparatory for the path of schooling, but also as accompanying and supporting measures while following this path. In this sense the name parallel or subsidiary exercises, as he sometimes refers to this group of exercises, is fitting. The German *Nebenübungen,* literally means parallel exercises; they have their place adjacent to the main exercises: the meditations that lead to the perception of metaphysical realities. Why is that so?

The spiritual schooling path is not without problems or dangers. This is what Rudolf Steiner was hinting at when he wrote in *How to Know Higher Worlds* (p. 4): 'What is essential does not lie in any single truth, but in the agreement between all. This process must be taken especially seriously by anyone carrying out the exercises. Although we may understand and practice an exercise correctly, this may yet have the wrong effect unless another exercise is added to it to resolve the one-sidedness of the first into harmony in the soul.'

The main exercises, the meditations, aim to make the soul independent of the body, in such a way that the soul can relate to the metaphysical world outside. In other words, it has an 'excarnating' effect. This brings problems with it. A danger can be to become estranged from daily life; or qualities may surface that distance us from other people, like vanity, dominance, egoism and untruthfulness, without our being aware of this. These negative motions of the soul can rise from the depth of our being if we are not completely present.

The meditations aim at a body-free consciousness: to excarnate without losing consciousness. The parallel exercises have a complementing, incarnating effect, restoring a healthy balance, because doing these exercises we have to be fully present all the time with our attention focused on a concrete, earthly situation. Controlling our thinking, the first exercise, focuses on tangible objects. The following exercise, controlling the will, is concerned with physical actions. Equanimity in the world of feeling, positivity and open-mindedness are all tested everyday life.

The effect of these exercises, if we do them over a long period of time, is such that even our unconscious is influenced. It is not just the soul that changes through this practicing activity, but also a deeper layer: the area of the life forces or the etheric body. This is the area into which our experiences sink when we 'forget' them and where the early development of our habits takes place. Habits lie in all sorts of fields: in the sphere of the physical activity (like the habit that we shake hands with our right hand), but also in the way we react to events. When habits take up a permanent place in the soul, we speak of 'character'. Rudolf Steiner recommended doing the parallel exercises for at least a month each time. That is the time needed to form a new habit. If we have practised something for four to six weeks, it becomes automatic; it surfaces from our unconscious, appearing without being called. If we live in this way with the exercises, they become 'characteristics' or 'virtues'; they become part of our character.

Consequently the inner harmony, to which the joining of the five separate exercises eventually leads, has an effect on the organism of the life forces. It is well known that the soul influences the state of the body. We usually know this in a negative way. An inner restlessness can eat away at us, causing weight loss; constant aggravation or bitterness affect the stomach and bile, and so on. Psychosomatic medicine is based on this. Recently a parallel science has arisen: psychoneuroimmunology (PNI). This new branch of medicine has found that people's attitude plays an essential role in mobilising defence mechanisms and healing forces. It is well known that the recovery chances of tuberculosis patients strongly increased if they looked to the future with confidence. The course of malignant and degenerative illnesses is also determined by whether the patients anticipated a task or a purpose in life. PNI confirmed these experiences.

People's attitude can then change physical substance, like immunoproteins, cholesterol, as well as antibodies. Our inner development, the harmonisation of our soul, is then echoed in the harmonising of the life forces. The first motive of beginning on a path of self-development, the wish to become healthy inside, shows a surprisingly profound perspective.

Exercises of the twelve-petalled lotus flower

In *How to Know Higher Worlds* the exercises of the sixfold path are given a special place. They are described as a part of the spiritual path of schooling; this part specifically helps develop a distinct inner organ whose structure becomes clearer as schooling progresses. The soul organ gains of mobility and structure. The effect of the exercises and meditations cause certain parts of the astral or soul body to become organs of perception: the lotus flowers or chakras. These organs are present in every person in a rudimentary form. By schooling them, they begin to develop and function, serving to perceive the spiritual environment.

Steiner describes first, in the chapter 'Some Effects of Initiation', the eight exercises that develop the sixteen-petalled lotus flower in the vicinity of the larynx. From the sixth century BC these have been known as the eightfold path of Buddha. This path seeks to develop following capacities:

Right perception
Right decision
Right word
Right action
Right structuring of life
Right striving
Right memory
Right reflection

Following this — in slightly changed sequence and with different nuances — there are the six exercises that are the subject of this booklet. They develop the twelve-petalled lotus flower in the region of the heart. The twelve-petalled lotus flower is the organ that perceives the intention, the inner mood of other souls. This can be experienced as soul warmth or coldness of soul. Also certain forces in animals and plants are perceived with this.

The six exercises are described as follows in *How to Know Higher Worlds*:

1. Control of thoughts
2. Control of actions
3. Cultivating perseverance
4. Forbearance or tolerance
5. Openness and impartiality (trust, confidence)
6. Equanimity

By comparison I will show the exercises as referred to in this book and in *An Outline of Esoteric Science*:

1. Control of thinking
2. Control of action or will impulses
3. Composure of feelings
4. Positivity

5. Open-mindedness or receptivity

6. Combining the preceding into harmony

In *How to Know Higher Worlds* there are six exercises, while in *An Outline of Esoteric Science* there are five exercises and a last all-encompassing exercise.

In *How to Know Higher Worlds* the second and the third exercises are both exercises of the will. The will is emphasised here. The sixth exercise has more of a feeling character to it. It is the last exercise of the series, as if it were the culmination. Feeling makes us perceive the relationship we have with the world around. Obviously the exercises in this book have a more social dimension directed into the world. The first exercise, control of thinking, for instance, is not just a matter of thinking in a controlled and objective way, but also quietly correcting any illogical thoughts of others. The fourth exercise, exercising tolerance of other people, beings and situations, goes a step further than exercising positivity, the fourth exercise in *How to Know Higher Worlds*. Also the fifth exercise, having trust and confidence in others, emphasises the social dimension. Trust is more than having an open mind.

So the exercises in *How to Know Higher Worlds* have a more outwardly oriented character leading to a new relationship to the world, while those in *An Outline of Esoteric Science* are more inwardly directed, toward a consolidation of the soul. But the most important difference is that both series of exercises occupy a completely different place in the schooling path.

The higher self

It is evident that the sixfold exercises in *An Outline of Esoteric Science* have the status of parallel exercises. Rudolf Steiner reaffirms the complementary value of these exercises. The longer we have practiced, the more our inner life becomes independent of what is happening in the world around. Our consciousness is then no longer dependent on external stimuli. There comes a time when our inner being has developed sufficient strength and wakefulness, that it can exist as a being in its own right in the spiritual world. In *An Outline of Esoteric Science* Rudolf Steiner describes how this being is experienced as a newly born second self existing alongside the customary self. It is with this second self that we can perceive and gain insight into higher worlds.

The ordinary self and the higher self are not unrelated. The forces absorbed by the higher self are drawn from the ordinary self. So it is vital that in everyday life the ordinary self must develop and maintain soul qualities ('virtues') even if we no longer work on developing these qualities continuously, for instance how truthful we are, how firm our character is or how strong our moral judgment. The purpose of the parallel exercises is to mobilise so much inner strength and to maintain it, so that a reliable higher development is possible.

Before giving the description of the sixfold path, in *An Outline of Esoteric Science* Rudolf Steiner wrote that seeking to control thinking, feeling and will serves a dual purpose. 'On the one hand, this practice is meant to imbue the soul with stability, certainty, and equilibrium to the extent that it retains these qualities even when a second 'I' is born out of it. On the other hand, it is meant to give this second 'I' strength and support for its journey.'

On the one hand we are working on making the soul healthy through the exercises, and on the other hand qualities are made available forces are given to the second self for the development of the heart lotus flower.

It is clear that the exercises of the sixfold path play a central role in the schooling path. Initially, they create the basis on which to build further inner development. In that sense, they are literally *basic exercises*. If we have also meditated as part of our inner activities, they help to maintain a healthy balance and counter the one-sidedness that can occur through meditation;

that is, of becoming too disconnected from the physical world and socially alienated. There they serve as *parallel exercises,* complementing the main (meditation) exercises. And thirdly, the sixfold exercises contribute to developing of the *twelve-petalled lotus flower,* the spiritual organ of perception located near the heart. When inner development reaches the point that we awaken to the spiritual world, then this second self can use the forces we have developed on the sixfold path to help the heart lotus flower to blossom. Through this the attitude of the *other* can be perceived spiritually.

The exercises can continually accompany us on our path of schooling. Their function and the way they work will change from step to step.

10. Working in Groups with the Basic Exercises

10. Working in Groups with the Basic Exercises

The basic exercises can be explored with others in a group to share their experience. At the beginning of the project it is useful to meet once a week. Once each exercise has been discussed, meeting once a month is a good rhythm.

The group can have a reasonable size with twenty to thirty participants. When exchanging experiences it will be helpful to split up into smaller groups. Experience shows that a smaller group of five to six people is the best size, as this allows raising more intimate problems and experiences, and gives each of the participants a chance to speak. In the larger group special hints and small 'discoveries' can be mentioned, questions can be asked and plans made for the period between meetings.

Specific questions are often helpful to give some direction to the discussion in the smaller groups. The following questions have been fruitful in practice.

The thinking exercise

> Which object did the various participants choose? (It is possible to do this exercise jointly with the help of a suitable object.)
> How did you move from the observing to the thinking?
> Which questions did you have concerning the object?
> Did you find any memory aids?
> Did you observe any changes in yourself?

Controlling the will

Which 'discoveries' have you made while looking for
an activity of your own?
How did you give this meaning for yourself?
What did you do if you missed the agreed time?
At which time of day did you plan to perform the
activity?
Which aids did you use to increase the likelihood of
success?
How did you feel if you succeeded in doing the
exercise?

The feeling exercise

How did you manage with mapping your feelings on a
chart?
Could you give a name to the feelings you found?
Did the layout of your feelings change as the days
passed?
Did you use the 'looking back' exercise for this
exercise?
Did that lead to something?
Did you manage to adequately express your feelings?
Did it lead to something if you expressed your feelings
more frequently?
Were you able to encounter the feelings of others in a
free and creative way?
Did you help them express their feelings?
Did something change in the relationship between
loud and quiet feelings?
What was the effect of this exercise on your inner life?

Positivity

For the first five minutes each participant in the smaller groups thinks of a difficult situation of the previous day. Could you see anything positive at the time? Then you tell the others about it. Sometimes in a negative situation you can find something positive immediately, but often some time has to pass before a positive aspect becomes visible.

Can you find examples of both situations?

Is there a difference in how the two work?

Does something change within you during this exercise?

Did you use the 'looking back' exercise when doing this exercise?

Were there any other ways to get make the positivity exercise more accessible?

Is it possible to use the exercise in a group (for instance, as a teacher talking with parents about their child, or a business meeting or something similar)?

Can you also detect a major talent in a troublesome child?

Having an open mind

What are the things that make your prejudiced, or worse, keep you imprisoned?

Is there something you can do to become more open-minded?

During the 'looking back' exercise (which is vital for this exercise) did you find anything that you did not notice initially?

For instance, which 'wonder' happened yesterday?

Were you able to embark on an adventure in a certain activity, such as a lesson or a conversation, and letting go of what you already knew?
Could you change or adapt your own planning?
Which changes took place within you during this exercise?

Harmony

Are there certain combinations of exercises that are obvious to do?
Did you find any aspects that made doing several exercises on one day fruitful?
What happened when you began this sixth exercise?

Excerpts from Rudolf Steiner's Books

Rudolf Steiner described these in a number of lectures and wrote about them in four places. The first time was in *How to Know Higher Worlds,* the second in a slightly modified form in *The Stages of Higher Knowledge.* Both books were based on articles originally written in 1904 and 1905 for the magazine, *Lucifer-Gnosis.*

In 1905 Steiner wrote about these exercises for students of the Esoteric School (which continued to the outbreak of the First World War). These writings were purely for the personal use of the students, though this text is now published in *Guidance in Esoteric Training.* Finally in 1909 the exercises were described in *An Outline of Esoteric Science.* This version could be seen as a final one.

Here we reprint this text from *An Outline of Esoteric Science* first, followed by the excerpt from *How to Know Higher Worlds.* The texts are reproduced by kind permission of SteinerBooks, USA.

1. How to Know Higher Worlds (pp. 118–22)

The twelve-petalled lotus flower, near the heart, is formed in a way similar to the sixteen-petalled one. Half of its petals were also already present and active in a past evolutionary stage of humanity. Thus, we do not have to develop those six petals; they appear on their own and begin to rotate when we start working on the other six petals. To promote their development, we must again deliberately orient certain soul activities in a particular direction.

We have to realise that the perceptions provided by the various spiritual or soul senses differ in character. The twelve-petalled lotus flower conveys a different perception from the sixteen-petalled one. The sixteen-petalled flower perceives forms. That is, it perceives as a form both another soul's way of thinking and the laws according to which a natural phenomenon unfolds. Such forms are not rigid and unmoving, but mobile and filled with life. A seer who has developed this sense organ can describe — for every way of thinking and natural law — the particular shape in which the thinking or law expresses itself. For example, a vengeful thought has an arrowlike and jagged shape, while a kind thought often has the form of a flower beginning to blossom, and so on. Thoughts that are firm and meaningful are symmetrical and regular; concepts that are unclear have wavy, almost frizzy outlines.

Quite different perceptions come to light through the twelve-petalled lotus flower. These may be roughly characterised in terms of warmth and coldness of soul. Seers, endowed with this sense organ, feel soul warmth or coldness streaming from the figures perceived by the sixteen-petalled lotus flower. This means that a seer who has developed the sixteen-petalled lotus flower, but not the twelve-petalled one, clairvoyantly perceives a kind thought only in terms of its figures described above. If, on the other hand, both organs are developed, then the seer also perceives something — that can be described only as soul warmth —streaming from the thought.

In esoteric schooling one sense organ is never developed apart from the others. The sense organs are always developed together. The above example, therefore, was given only hypothetically, for the sake of clarity.

Developing the twelve-petalled lotus flower gives us profound insight into the processes of nature. Everything growing and maturing radiates soul warmth, while everything undergoing death, destruction, and decay has the quality of soul coldness.

The twelve-petalled lotus flower is formed in the following way.

First, we pay attention to directing the sequence of our thoughts — this is the so-called 'practice of the control of thoughts'. Just as thinking true and meaningful thoughts develops the sixteen-petalled lotus flower, so inwardly controlling our thinking processes develops the twelve-petalled flower. Thoughts that flit about like will-o'-the-wisps and follow each other by chance rather than in a logical, meaningful way distort and damage the form of this flower. The more logically our thoughts follow one another and the more we avoid all illogical thinking, the more perfectly this organ develops its proper form.

Therefore whenever we hear an illogical thought, we should immediately allow the correct thought to pass through our mind. But, if we find ourselves in what seems an illogical environment, we should not for that reason unlovingly withdraw in order to further our development. By the same token, we should not feel the immediate urge to correct any illogicality we witness around us. Rather, we should inwardly and very quietly give the thoughts rushing at us from the outside a logical and meaningful direction. We should always strive to maintain this logical direction in our own thinking.

Second, we must bring an equally logical consistency into our actions — this is the practice of the control of actions. Any instability and disharmony in our actions injures the development of the twelve-petalled lotus flower. Therefore, each of our actions should follow logically from whatever action came before. If we act today out of different principles than we did yesterday, we shall never develop the lotus flower in question.

Third, we must cultivate perseverance. As long as we consider a goal we have set ourselves to be right and worthy, we should never let any outside influence deter us from striving to reach it. We should consider obstacles as challenges to be overcome, not as reasons, for giving up.

Fourth, we must develop forbearance (or tolerance) toward other people, other beings, and events. We must suppress all unnecessary criticism of imperfection, evil, and wickedness and seek rather to understand everything that comes to meet us. Just as the sun does not withdraw its light from wickedness and evil, so we, too, should not withdraw our understanding and sympathy from anyone. When we meet adversity, we should not indulge in negative judgments but accept the inevitable and try, as best we can, to turn it to the good. Similarly, instead of considering the opinions of others only from our own standpoint, we should try to put ourselves into their position.

Fifth, we must develop openness and impartiality toward all the phenomena of life. This is sometimes called faith or trust. We must learn to approach every person, every being, with trust. Such trust or confidence must inspire all our actions. We should never say, in reply to something said to us, 'I don't believe that because it contradicts the opinion I have already formed'. Rather, when faced with something new, we must always be willing to test our opinions and views and revise them if necessary. We must always remain receptive to whatever approaches us. We should trust in the effectiveness of whatever we undertake. All doubt and timidity should be banished from our being. If we have a goal, we must have faith in the power of our goal. Even a hundred failures should not be able to take this faith from us. This is the 'faith that can move mountains'.

Sixth, we must achieve a certain balance in life (or serenity). As esoteric students, we should strive to maintain a mood of inner harmony whether joy or sorrow comes to meet us. We should lose the habit of swinging between being 'up one minute and down the next'. Instead, we should be as prepared to deal with misfortune and danger as with joy and good fortune.

The reader familiar with spiritual scientific literature will recognise in the practice of these six qualities the so-called 'six attributes' that a person seeking initiation has to develop. They are mentioned now because of their relationship to the development of the sense organ of the soul called the twelve-petalled lotus flower.

2. An Outline of Esoteric Science (pp. 310–16)

An appropriate training lists certain qualities that those who want to find the way into the higher world should acquire through practice. These are, above all, the soul's mastery over its train of thought, its will, and its feelings. The method for bringing this mastery about through practice has two goals. On the one hand, this practice is meant to imbue the soul with stability, certainty, and equilibrium to the extent that it retains these qualities even when a second I is born out of it. On the other hand, it is meant to give this second I strength and support for its journey.

Objectivity is what our thinking needs most of all for spiritual training. In the physical world of the senses, life is the great teacher of the human I as far as objectivity is concerned. If the soul chose to allow its thoughts to wander aimlessly, it would have to be immediately corrected by life so as not to come into conflict with it. The soul's thinking must correspond to the actual course of life's realities. When we turn our attention away from the physical world of the senses, we are no longer subject to its automatic correction, so our thinking will go astray if it is not able to self-correct. This is why students of the spirit must train their thinking so that it can set its own direction and goals. Their thinking must teach itself inner stability and the ability to stick strictly to one subject. For this reason, the appropriate 'thought exercises' we undertake should not deal with unfamiliar and complicated objects, but with ones that are simple and familiar.

Over a matter of months, if we can overcome ourselves to the point of being able to focus our thoughts for at least five minutes a day on some ordinary object (for example, a pin, a pencil, or the like), and if, during this time, we exclude all thoughts unrelated to this object, we will have made a big step in the right direction. (We can consider a new object each day or stay with the same one for several days.) Even those who consider themselves thinkers because of their scientific education should not scorn this means of preparing themselves for spiritual training, because if we fix our thoughts on something very familiar for a certain period of time, we can be certain that we are thinking objectively. If we ask: What is a pencil made of? How are these materials prepared? How are they put together to make pencils? When were pencils invented? and so on, our thoughts correspond to reality much more closely than they do if we think about the origin of human beings or the nature of life. Simple thought exercises are better for developing objective thinking about the Saturn, Sun, and Moon phases of evolution than any complicated scholarly ideas, because what we think about is not the point, at least initially. The point is to think objectively, using our own inner strength. Once we have taught ourselves objectivity by practicing on sense-perceptible physical processes that are easily surveyed, our thinking becomes accustomed to striving for objectivity even when it does not feel constrained by the physical world of the senses and its laws. We break ourselves of the habit-of allowing our thoughts to wander without regard for the facts.

The soul must become a ruler in the domain of the will just as it is in the world of thoughts. Here again, life itself appears as the controlling element in the physical world of the senses. It makes us need certain things, and our will feels roused to satisfy these needs. For the sake of higher training, we must get used to strictly obeying our own commands. If we do this, we will become less and less inclined to desire nonessentials. Dissatisfaction and instability in our life of will, however, are based on desiring things without having any clear concept of realising these desires. This dissatisfaction can disrupt our entire mental life when a higher I is trying to emerge from the soul.

A good exercise is to tell ourselves to do something daily at a specific time, over a number of months: Today at this particular time I will do *this*. We then gradually become able to determine what to do and when to do it in a way that makes it possible to carry out the action in question with great precision. In this way, we rise above damaging thoughts, such as: 'I'd like this, I want to do that', which disregard totally the feasibility of what we want. A very great man put these words into the mouth of a seer: 'I love whomever longs for the impossible'.[1] This great man himself said, 'Living in ideas means treating the impossible as if it were possible'.[2] These statements, however, should not be used as objections to what has been presented here, because what Goethe and his seeress Manto ask can only be accomplished by those who have trained themselves in desiring what is possible in order to then be able to apply their strong will to 'impossibilities' in a way that transforms them into possibilities.

For the sake of spiritual training, the soul should also acquire a certain degree of composure with regard to the domain of feeling. For this to happen, the soul must master its expressions of joy and sorrow, pleasure and pain. There are many prejudices that become evident with regard to acquiring this particular quality. We might imagine that we would become dull and unreceptive to the world around us if we are not meant to empathise with rejoicing or pain. However, that is not the point. The soul should indeed rejoice when there is reason to rejoice, and it should feel pain when something sad happens. It is only meant to master its *expressions* of joy and sorrow, of pleasure and displeasure. With this as our goal, we will soon notice that rather than becoming dulled to pleasurable and painful events in our surroundings, the opposite is true. We are becoming more receptive to these things than we were previously. Admittedly, acquiring this character trait requires strict self-observation over a long period of time. We must make sure that we are able to empathise fully with joy and sorrow without losing ourselves and expressing our feelings involuntarily. What we are meant

1   Goethe, *Faust*, Part Two, Act 2.
2   Goethe, *Verses in Prose*.

to suppress is not our justified pain, but involuntary weeping; not our abhorrence of a misdeed, but blind rage; not alertness to danger, but fruitless fear, and so on.

Exercises like this are the only way for students of the spirit to acquire the mental tranquillity that is needed to prevent the soul from leading a second, unhealthy life, like a shadowy double, alongside the higher I when this I is born and especially when it begins to be active, Especially with regard to these things, it is important not to succumb to self-deception. It can easily seem to people that they already possess a certain equilibrium in ordinary life and that they therefore do not need this exercise, but in fact it is doubly necessary for people like this. It's quite possible to be calm and composed in confronting things in ordinary life and yet have our suppressed lack of equilibrium assert itself all the more when we ascend into a higher world. It is essential to realise that for purposes of spiritual training, what we seem to possess already is much less important than systematically practicing what we need to acquire. This sentence is quite correct, regardless of how contradictory it may seem. No matter what life may have taught us, *what we teach ourselves* is what serves the purposes of spiritual training. If life has taught us excitability we need to break that habit, but if it has taught us complacency we need to shake ourselves up through self-education so that our souls' reactions correspond to the impressions they receive. People who cannot laugh at anything have as little control over their lives as people who are constantly provoked to uncontrollable laughter.

An additional way of training our thinking and feeling is by acquiring a quality we can call 'positivity'. There is a beautiful legend that tells of Christ Jesus and several other people walking past a dead dog.[1] The others all turned away from the ugly sight, but Christ Jesus spoke admiringly of the animal's beautiful teeth. We can practice maintaining the soul-attitude toward

---

1   A story attributed to the Persian poet Nizami (1141–1203), and adapted by Goethe for inclusion in his *West-östlicher Divan*. It is translated into English as 'Agraphon' in *Selected Poems,* Angelos Sikelianos, Princeton University Press, Princeton, 1979, pp. 137–39.

the world that this legend exemplifies. The erroneous, the bad, and the ugly must not prevent the soul from finding the true, the good, and the beautiful wherever they are present. We must not confuse this positivity with being artificially uncritical or arbitrarily closing our eyes to things that are bad, false, or inferior. It is possible to admire a dead animal's 'beautiful teeth' and still see the decaying corpse; the corpse does not prevent us from seeing the beautiful teeth. We cannot consider bad things good and false things true, but we can reach the point where the bad does not prevent us from seeing the good and errors do not keep us from seeing the truth.

Our thinking undergoes a certain maturing process in connection with the will when we attempt never to allow anything we have experienced to deprive us of our unbiased receptivity to new experiences. For students of the spirit, the thought: 'I've never heard of that; I don't believe it', should totally lose its meaning. During specific periods of time, we should be intent on using every opportunity to learn something new concerning every thing and every being. If we are ready and willing to take previously unaccustomed points of view, we can learn from every current of air, every leaf, every babbling baby. Admittedly, it is easy to go too far with regard to this ability. At any given stage in life, we should not disregard all our previous experiences. We should indeed judge what we are experiencing in the present on the basis of past experiences. This belongs on one side of the scales; on the other, however, students of the spirit must place their inclination to constantly experience new things and especially their faith in the possibility that new experiences will contradict old ones.

We have now listed five soul qualities that students in a genuine spiritual training need to acquire: control of one's train of thought, control of one's will impulses, composure in the face of joy and sorrow, positivity in judging the world, and receptivity in one's attitude toward life. Having spent certain periods of time practicing these qualities consecutively, we will then need to bring them into harmony with each other in our souls. We will need to practice them in pairs, or in combinations of three and one at the same time, and so on, in order to bring about this harmony.

Notes

Lusseyran, Jacques, *Against the Pollution of the I* (published in UK as *What One Sees Without Eyes)* Parabola, New York 1999.

—, *Le monde commence aujourd'hui* (The world begins today) Table ronde, Mayenne 1959

—, *What One Sees Without Eyes,* (published in USA as *Against the Pollution of the I)* Floris Books, Edinburgh 1999.

Maslow, Abraham, *Motivation and Personality,* Longman Asia, Hong Kong 1987.

Romunde, Dick van, *About Formative Forces in the Plant World,* Jannebeth Roel 2001.

Saint-Exupéry, Antoine de, *The Little Prince,* Egmont 1991.

Steiner, Rudolf, *Guidance in Esoteric Training. From the Esoteric School* (Collected Works (CW) No. 245), Rudolf Steiner Press, UK 2001.

—, *How to Know Higher Worlds. A Modern Path of Initiation* (CW 10, also published as *Knowledge of the Higher Worlds),* SteinerBooks, USA 1994.

—, *Knowledge of the Higher Worlds and its Attainment* (CW 10, also published as *How to Know Higher Worlds),* Rudolf Steiner Press, UK 2006.

—, *The Stages of Higher Knowledge* (CW 12), SteinerBooks, USA 2009.

—, *Theosophy. An Introduction to the Spiritual Processes in Human Life and in the Cosmos* (CW 9) SteinerBooks, USA 1994.